**Collected
Poems**

**Collected
Poems**
John Berger

STACK
BOOKS

Smokestack Books
PO Box 408, Middlesbrough TS5 6WA
e-mail: info@smokestack-books.co.uk
www.smokestack-books.co.uk

Collected Poems
copyright 2014, John Berger, all rights reserved.
Original monoprints: Yves Berger

Cover image: Yves Berger
Author portrait: Jules Linglin

ISBN 978-0-9927409-5-5

Smokestack Books is represented
by Inpress Ltd

To Beverly,
mistress of each page.

Contents

Monotype drawings by Yves Berger

Words

Words I

for Beverly

Down the gorge
      ran
           people and blood

In the bracken
      beyond touch
         a dog howled

A head between lips
      opened
           the mouth of the world

Her breasts
      like doves
          perch on her ribs

Her child sucks the long
      white thread
          of words to come

Words II

The tongue
     is the spine's first leaf
forests of language surround it

Like a mole
     the tongue
burrows through the earth of speech

Like a bird
     the tongue
flies in arcs of the written word

The tongue is tethered and alone in its mouth

1980

Pages

Word by word I describe
you accept each fact
and ask yourself:
what does he really mean?

Quarto after quarto of sky
salt sky
sky of the placid tear
printed from the other sky
punched with stars.
Pages laid out to dry.

Birds like letters fly away
O let us fly away
circle and settle on the water
near the fort of the illegible.

1972

A Song for Tom

Friday night drives Monday crazy
Shit for five days out of seven
Sunshine tonight unzip your heaven

Friday night drives Monday crazy

Squeeze my lemon no end to fear
'Cos you and I we'll stay here
If Friday night drives Monday crazy

1990s

A Dream Which I Inscribed Verbatim

Not the horse run wild
nor the men on their feet dismounted
could lead her through the wood to believe
      that he had truly died.

O bite the lobe of his ear, they said
And draw the bolt of his life.

There at the end of the green leafed ride
they hanged him on a holly holly tree
And she wept 'til her tears rolled stones
      down my mountain side.

1960

A Letter

A sailor receives a letter
from a thousand versts away.
His wife has written
that in their house
beyond the cliffs
she is happy.

And this *is* of her letter
during evenings with girls
in untranslatable ports
through the sea of the months
persuades the cursing sailor
that his never-ending voyage
will end.

1979

Orchard

On my way to the sea
I passed an orchard

the branches of the trees
exposed to the prevailing
sea wind
were tangled

likewise their shadows

that day there was no wind

the cows in the orchard
twitched their flanks in the sunlight
to disturb the flies

in the tangled shadows daisies
made me imagine
how a grain of sand might open
and white petals radiate
from the opened yellow grain

the late blossom on a tree
at the orchard's edge
was the colour of my brain
white rose with flecks of light and blood

thoughts in a brain
stay invisible
hence words to reveal.

I thought:
every day this orchard
is part of
        a gale.

1972

The Unsaid

On my table
a pile of letters
not yet replied to
the earliest dated
three years before.
One evening I decide
the time has come
to deal with them all.
Letters from poets
more lyrical than I
requesting advice,
letters from institutions
inviting me to speak
on communication
or the use of art...
from an insurance company
a reminder explaining
I had overlooked
the obligatory premium
against natural disasters,
a birthday card.

Among the post unanswered
two letters
from close friends.
The handwritings,
one fat and one thin,
not easy to decipher,
yet over the years
I had read them avidly
finding encouragement.

Now both are dead
their last letters
lost in a pile:
both killed themselves
one with a gun
one in a canal.

1985

Pen Pencil and a Rubber

As I went home
      on the suburban train
nothing in the world yet had an end
            books to read
            men's tricks
            the reaches of philosophy
            Mother's sewing
            the KGB
            and the things I could do to my hair

As I walked through the night
      from the station
I made an inventory of what I was waiting for
            a post as a teacher
            next Sunday off
            communism
            a husband
            my new winter coat
            and poems not yet written

Before I undressed
      and lay down in bed
I checked what I'd need next day
            my notes on Hegel
            a slice of koulibek
            enough lined paper with a margin
            seeds to feed the birds
            pen pencil
            and a rubber.

1980s

Viva Voce

One who dreams deeply
of mountains
speaks next day
with the voice of a bureaucrat

Another whom nobody dares disturb
sleeping like a tank
parked in a square
will plead with the voice of a child
that he was never disobedient

A third to overcome insomnia
imagines himself a beaver
and barks at meetings
in the name of necessity

He whose nightmares
are of history being unchangeable
will explain like a teacher
precisely what is needed
in order to progress

Into the ear of the poem
I write these riddles
never spoken
viva voce

1970s

Story Tellers

Writing
crouched beside death
we are his secretaries

Reading by the candle of life
we complete his ledgers

Where he ends,
my colleagues,
we start, either side of the corpse

And when we cite him
we do so
for we know the story is almost over.

1984

October

Perhaps God resembles the story tellers
loving the feeble more than
the strong
the victors less
than the stricken.
Either way
in weak late October
the forest burns
with the sunshine
of the whole vanished summer.

2004

Leavings

Brightest guests have gone
Green furnishings are down,
Shadeless light condones
Black frost on window panes.

Where lovers and grasses
Spent their seeds
Over iron crevices
Ice now makes the beds.

Yet indulge no regret.
Mouse eye of robin,
Creeping silence,
These cautious lines,

Bear witness still
In their circumvention
To the constant
Tenancy of man.

1956/57

Migrant Words

In a pocket of the earth
I buried all the accents
of my mother tongue

there they lie
like needles of pine
assembled by ants

one day the stumbling cry
of another wanderer
may set them alight

then warm and comforted
he will hear all night
the truth as lullaby

1980

Napalm

Mother let me cry
not letterpress
nor telex
nor stainless speech
bulletins
announce disaster
with impunity –
but the pages of the wound.

Mother let me speak
not adjectives
to colour
their maps of wretchedness
nor nouns to classify
the families of pain –
but the verb of suffering.

My mother tongue taps
the sentence
on the prison wall
Mother let me write
the voices
howling in the falls.

1991

History

Requiem

Green
fills
the earth's two breasts
day and night
trees of the forest
suckle green.
Of all the colours
green is the last.

Wind
dries the soil
powdery and light
in the deepest clay
stains
the brown of blood
repeatedly dried
die again
as the wind drops
under the rain.

Green
unlike silver or red
I say to you Nella
is never still
green who waited
mineral ages
for the leaf
is the colour of their souls
and comes as gift.

1986

16.45h The Firing Squad

The dog carried the day in her mouth
over the fields of the small hours
towards a hiding place
which before had been safe.

Nobody was woken before dawn.

At noon
the dog sprawling in the shade
placed the pup between her four paws
and waited in vain
for it to suck.

A line of prisoners
hands knotted
fall forward
into the grave they have dug.

Belly to the earth
the dog carries the day
which has never stirred
back to its dark.

Under the stars the bereaved
imagine they hear
a dog howling too
on the edge of the world.

This piteous day was born
stone-deaf and blind.

1991

History

The pulse of the dead
        as interminably
constant as the silence
which pockets the thrush.

The eyes of the dead
        inscribed on our palms
as we walk on this earth
which pockets the thrush.

1980s

Two Poems of the Taiga

for Nella

I

Perhaps our sledge is made of its speed
your outstretched hand our blanket
a foreign language learnt at night
      the track we take
           between the trees.

You have filled the thermos with coffee
packed our footprints if needed
to throw into the jaws
      of the untestifying
           ravenous snow.

Together like carpenters with hammers
we have taught the distance
how to build a roof
      from the trees
           we fly between.

In the silence left behind
I no longer hear the far away
question of the summer house:
      and tomorrow
           where shall we go?

At dusk the harnessed dogs fear
there's no end to the forest
and in the snow every night
      we calm them
           with our surprising laughter.

II

In the undergrowth
     lights a hammered nail
in the undergrowth
     words are spoken by the dead
in the undergrowth
     the news is of prison
knowing the worst
     the undergrowth chose us.

In the undergrowth
     from wild boars we learnt tact
in the undergrowth
     we read the frost of stars
carrying the undergrowth
     we heated ovens for bread
knowing the worst
     we chose the undergrowth.

You from the plain
     I from the sea
we recalled horizons.
     Or did we foresee them
in the undergrowth
     where you and I slept
in each other's arms
     like forsaken skies?

1980

Self-portrait 1914-18

It seems now that I was so near to that war.
I was born eight years after it ended
When the General Strike had been defeated.

Yet I was born by Very Light and shrapnel
On duck boards
Among limbs without bodies.

I was born of the look of the dead
Swaddled in mustard gas
And fed in a dugout.

I was the groundless hope of survival
With mud between finger and thumb
Born near Abbeville.

I lived the first year of my life
Between the leaves of a pocket bible
Stuffed in a khaki haversack.

I lived the second year of my life
With three photos of a woman
Kept in a standard issue army paybook.

In the third year of my life
At 11am on November 11th 1918
I became all that was conceivable.

Before I could see
Before I could cry out
Before I could go hungry

I was the world fit for heroes to live in.

1970

Trilling

The canary sings inside the eagle
and is mad.
The canary sings inside the cage
of the eagle's breast.
The slow beat of the eagle's wings
accelerated
flows like an incessant giggle
musically
from the canary's quivering beak.
The canary trills highest
when the eagle kills.

1972

Mostar

for Simon and Lilo

On the Saturday mornings
reduced now to dust
on the Saturday mornings
of weeks which had
seven normal days
and seven quiet nights
unless we drank
on the Saturday mornings
I'd carry out to the balcony
my shoes
and a pair or two of hers
she had fourteen pairs or more
on the balcony on the fifth floor
my finger wrapped in a scrap of rag
circling the tin of polish
balanced on the balustrade
I applied the black
to the little sides
the snub toe
the slender heel
whose tip was no longer than a dice
for her right foot and left
then I'd leave them a moment
saying to myself
it does good
to let the wax feed the leather
before taking the brush
and with two fingers of the other hand
poked in the toe
polishing them til they shone
on Saturday morning.

Now the brush
the fifth floor
her feet
all have vanished.

1995

For Howe 1909-1985

I know you
by my ignorance
and its space
which shyly
you filled with quotations

I know you
by the half smile of your reticence
and the space
of a pride
you hid in patched sleeves

I know you
by the moment before death
and the space
of God
you found in the lament of words

I know you
by your daughter
and the space
of the words
between here and then

18.7.85

On a Degas Bronze of a Dancer

You say the leg supports the body
But have you never seen
The seed in the ankle
   Whence the body grows?

You say (if you are the builder of bridges
I think you are) each pose
Must have its natural equilibrium
But have you never seen
Recalcitrant muscles of dancers
   Hold their unnatural own?

You say (if as rational
As I hope you are) the biped's evolution
Was accomplished long ago
But have you never seen
The still miraculous sign
A little in from the hip
Predicting nine inches below
   Bodies fork in two?

Then let us look together
(We who both know
Light's the go-between
Of space and time)
Let us look at this figure
To verify
   I my goddess
   And you the stress.

Think in terms of bridges.
See, the road of leg and back
Hingeing at hip and shoulder
Holds firm from palm to heel
Single leg as pier
Thigh above the knee
Cantilevering member.

Think in terms of bridges
Over what men once called Lethe.
See, the ordinary body we cross through
Vulnerable, inhabited, warm
Stands the strain too.
Dead Load, Live Load
And Longitudinal Drag.

So let the bridge this dancer arches for us
Stand the strain of all old prejudice
So let's verify again,
    You my goddess
    And I the stress.

1960

Ypres

Base: fields whose mud is waterlogged

Perpendicular: thin larches
                planted in rows
                    with broken
                        branches

Horizontal: brick walls the colour of
                dead horses

Sinking: lower
            and lower
                houses with dark windows

Sometimes a wall is white-washed
A rectangle of dead lime
                under the indifferent clouds

Chickens should have webbed feet here
At dusk drowned soldiers cross the fields to steal them

Through base
            perpendicular
            and horizontal
                there is order:
                the order of split wood
                broken branches
                walls the colour of dead horses
                and roofs fallen in

There is no way out except across
Nothing reaches any heaven from here

Between earth and sky there is
            a transparent canopy
            plaited from cock crows
            and the cries of soldiers

1973

History

Canopyless sky
regular as the sun
millennia powdered into blue
sky of all moments lived
sky I crane my neck to look into
sky of what I shall become
      in this sky
      two buzzards
      motionless
      bent necks
      heads intent
      like heads of turtles
      upside down
      wing tips ragged

(because wings permit flight
we imagine them immaculate)

      untidy
      disarranged
      with feathers missing
      lethargic
      heavy wings
      to support the intent head
      the yellow beak
      the gut demanding food
      talons that grip
      tear to shreds like judges

the upside-down-turtle-heads of two birds
turning as slowly as history
refusing motion
predatory
in the canopyless sky of moments lived
of millennia powdered into blue

Jura 1973

The Partisans of Cervignano

for Anya

Giorgione gave this light a name
In this evening light the awaited
Arrives like a god
From all directions at once.

In this evening light the awaited
Bears the weight of the tools
Off the shoulders
Of those walking home from the hills.

In this evening light the awaited
Expects to find
On a wooden table
Wine the colour of the moon.

In this evening light the awaited
Destroys all calculation,
Time and distance now no more
Than the stretching of desire.

In this evening light the awaited
Is reached
Like a bed in a prepared room
With a petal on the floor.

In this evening light the awaited
Will tell how in this light
Men I might have loved
Were shot, their desires unmet.

1958

Expulsion

The Adams and Eves
continually expelled
and with what tenacity
returning at night!

Before,
when the two of them
did not count
and there were no months
no births and no music
their fingers were unnumbered.

Before,
when the two of them did not count
did they feel
a prickling behind the eyes
a thirst in the throat
for something other than
the perfume of infinite flowers
and the breath of immortal animals?
In their untrembling sleep
did the tips of their tongues
seek the bud of another taste
which was mortal and sweating?

Did they envy the longing
of those to come after the Fall?

Women and men still return
to live through the night
all that uncounted time.

And with the punctuality
of the first firing squad
the expulsion is at dawn.

1980s

Born 5/11/26

Redder every day
the leaves of the pear trees.
Tell me what is bleeding.
Not summer
for summer left early.
Not the village
for the village though drunk on its road
has not fallen.
Not my heart
for my heart bleeds no more
than the arnica flower.

Nobody has died this month
or been fortunate enough
to receive a foreign work-permit.
We fed with soup
let sleep in the barn
no more thoughts of suicide
than is normal in November.
Tell me what is bleeding
you who see in the dark.

Hands of the world
amputated by profit
bleed in
streets of bloodsheds.

1983

Family Tree

You have unusually long arms
said the salesman
glad of the chance to use
fitting critical criteria
when I went to buy my coat.

Your arches are unusually high
said the woman
forty years ago
who came each week
to set my mother's hair
and knew a little chiropody.

An unusually strong jaw yours
said the Austrian dentist when
head back and mouth open
I let him extract a tooth
in North London.

Soon such attributes will be as
indistinguishable as particles
in the cloud of white dust
which settles on the grass
when the cart has passed
        cows grass
        grass of the neighbour's horse
        two sheeps grass
        fowls grass
        grass of four apple trees
        Serbian grass
        my ancestors scythed.

I have unusually long arms
their length
would have made scything easier.

1960s

For Those in Hiding

In the far away dawn shadows
on the western side of the trees
what a fear there was
of the day now begun
with the arrival of the sun.

2003

Jura Mountains

begins again with a rectangle
a table say
    with knives upon it
    and glaciers
    and the helmet of a white bull
lost in the snow

above this rectangle
he places another
    of a blue he can never touch
if he lays a finger on the skin of this blue
he will touch the moment of his own conception
and of the end of the world
    which begins with the sun

between these two rectangles
    what can he place?
here words ricochet off the snow
    as off gun metal

between these two rectangles
    in this poem he places
        two jays
          mating
    led by the mild season
to believe the time of abundance
        has come.

1960s

Seven Levels of Despair

To search each morning
to find the scraps
with which to survive another day.

The knowledge on waking
that in this legal wilderness
no rights exist.

The experience over the years
of nothing getting better
only worse.
The humiliation of being able
to change almost nothing,
and of seizing upon the almost
which then leads to another impasse.

The listening to a thousand promises
which pass inexorably
beside you and yours.

The example of those who resist
being bombarded to dust.

The weight of your own killed
a weight which closes
innocence for ever
because they are so many.

2001

Rembrandt Self-portrait

The eyes from the face
two nights looking at the day
the universe of his mind
doubled by pity
nothing else can suffice.
Before a mirror
silent as a horseless road
he envisaged us
deaf dumb
returning overland
to look at him
in the dark.

1975

Orlando Letelier 1932-1976

Once I will visit you
he said
in your mountains
today
assassinated
blown to pieces
he has come to stay
he lived in many places
and he died everywhere
in this room
he has come between the pages
of open books
there's not a single apple
on the trees
loaded with fruit this year
which he has not counted
apples the colour of gifts
he faces death no more
there's not a precipice
over which his corpse
has not been hurled
the silence of his voice
tidy and sweet as the leaf of a beech
will be safe in the forest
I never heard him speak
in his mother tongue
except when he named the names
of patriots
the clouds race over the grass
faster than sheep
never lost
he consulted the compass of his heart
always accurate
took bearings from the needle of Chile
and the eye of Santiago
through which he has now passed.

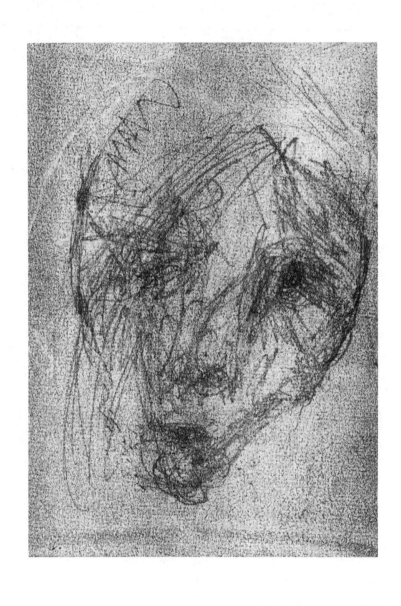

Emigration

Slavonski Brod

The wooden slav house
has double windows
so that winter cold
may not enter
put its hands on the table
its feet in the bed

in the summer and autumn
on the wooden sill
between the windows
flowers are regularly
watered in their pots
so that there is always colour
between kitchen
and garden

there too are kept
between the panes
the invisible keepsakes
of those who left.

1970s

Rural Emigration

Mornings are mothers
bringing up their pastures
drying invisible sheets
across the orchard
and teasing the steaming rocks
with tales of sun and bed

The evenings planted fences
watched the poultry
peck in the dog-high grass
gathered their bragging clouds
and thundered passion
to the feeding mothers

Day after day
morning and evening coupled
grass and leaves grew up
and the drenched green catkins
fell from our walnut tree
like dead caterpillars

1979

Memory of a Village Church

How to explain the world
with a rounded arch
cut like a melon
whose sweetness was a welcome?

The pews
were like seats in a wagon.

How to explain the world
with a Madonna painted blue
who knew no evil
and a devil whose horns
were invariably visible?

The wagon
was drawn by our prayers

we did not know
it would deposit us here.

1970s

The sky is blue black

The sky is blue black
starlings unfold their wings
quit their pediments
to write a letter
returned.
The setting sun
fills teeth with gold.
Like a shred of meat
I'm lodged in this town.

1970s

Their Railways

Keep tears
My heart
For prose.

Train
Flammes bleues
Fleurs jaunes.
In the ditches
I am water.
Between
Grow kingcups of your childhood.
Sunk in my eyes
Skies of the churchyard.
Through arteries
Of gravel
Whispering to my grasses
The blood of good-byes.
Flammes bleues
Fleurs jaunes
Their railways.

1985/86

Far Away

Was it my father
who laid this wood?

Is the hand
that strikes the match
        historic?

The wind cross-questioned
and the tongues of flame
replied.

The emigrant's fire.

On my knees
to balance the saucepan
kitchen mother
kerchief head
I recall you
and call you again

The poppies of your yard
are scattered in my clouds.

1975/76

Eight Poems of Emigration

I Village

I tell you
      all the houses
are holes in the arse of stone

we eat off coffin lids

between evening star
      and milk in a bucket
is nothing

the chum is emptied
      twice a day

cast us
      steaming
          on the fields.

II Earth

the purple scalp of the earth
combed in autumn
          and times of famine

the metal bones of the earth
          extracted by hand

the church above the earth
          arms of our clock crucified

all is taken

III Leaving

pain
cannot

endure long enough

tracks vanish
under snow
the white embrace
of leaving

I have tried to write the truth on trains

without an ear
the tongue takes fright
clings to a single word

the train is crossing a bridge
black ice collects
on each letter
S A V A
my river

IV Metropolis

the edge of moonlight
sharp
like the level
    of water in a canal

the locks of reason

at dawn
when the level of the dark
is brought down
    to that of the light

accept the dark
massed black
zone of blindness
accept it eyes

but here the dark
has been stolen in a sack
weighted down with a pebble
and drowned

there is no longer any dark

V Factory

here
it is dawn eternally
hour of awakening
hour of revolutionary prophesy
hour of the embers dead
time of the days work
without end

there we built the night
as we lit the fire
lay down in it
pulled up the dark as blanket

near fields were
the breath of animals asleep
quiet of the earth
warm as the fire

cold is the pain of believing
warmth will never return

here
night is time forgotten
eternal dawn
and in the cold I dream
          of how the pine
          burnt
          like a dog's tongue
          behind its teeth

VI Waterfront

all night Hudson
coughs in bed

I try to sleep

my country
is a hide nailed to wood

the wind of my soul rushes

out of horizons
I make a hammock

in sleep
I suck birth village
touch my river's curve

two black mackerel
pilot in
daybreak

gaff them sky gaff them

VII Absence

when the sun was no higher than the grass
jewels hung in the trees
and the terraces turned rose
between fluorescent lights along the ringroad
apartments hung their pietas

they are frying potatoes
a factory discharges its hands in woollen gloves
there is a hole in my thumb

the vines are not green
the vines are not here
the jewels
crushed in high voltage wires
will be worn by the dead
DANGER DE MORT

VIII A Forest I Knew

Let me die like this

the branches have muscles
        hills get up
the cloud pours
        into a cup

in the forest wild boar
        have eaten
        are warm
            and sleepy

each clearing is recorded
        on a screen I carry
rolled like a cloth
        in my head

a sheet
        pulled over
            the eyes of the dead
keeps out the look of the world
on the cloth
        unrolled
I follow their spoor
        in the forest I knew.

1980s

Postcard from Troy

In this metropolis
death wears a sheep skin

along the freeways
the traffic never stops

beneath the side street waterfall
three coffins full

baa baa black sheep

grass grows in the taxis

who can reverse
the hour glass of gravel?

to pin down
the wall to wall carpet
wood anemones are hammered in

yes sir yes sir
the gate is shut.

only enough to wrap
dead bunting in.

1990

Suicide

Pips of the full moon
spilt on the rooves
the childhood lamps
of my village

emptied
the moon was a dried
bleached apricot

to part

on nightshift
the wind is breathless
for the skies too
have silicosis

what is being cast in the sand?
I placed my ear
to the earth's rib
the silence of cement

if the moon is full
my heart
when we return
let us walk by the quarries
to look down
at where our body lies.

1977

Troy

This city is exceptional.
It was built vertically
and does not stand on the earth.
It grew like ivy on a wall.
We who live in it walk
up and down
with the ease of centipedes.
At right angles
to the plain and sea
we live on the walls of a shaft.
A river runs between our streets
like rain down bark.

The last day of the year
all cities have the right
to wear disguise.
With immunity Marrakech
can put on the clothes of Paris
Madrid can imagine itself free
Trinidad blow up the Bank of England.

This city invents for itself
a sky
unwinds it like a bale of cloth.

In a dream I found
a bird's egg the blue of the sky.
Where the blue joins the roofs of the street
it rattles inaudibly.
My eyes see the sound.

At the core of the sun
in the sky
the glacier of justice may attain
the speed of light
taking a month
to cross the solar system
or a hundred thousand years
to reach the farthest star
within our galaxy.

At the end of the street
a sparrow
perches high up against the sky
in a tree of veins
near the cortex.

When a prisoner is shot
the sparrow flies
out of his eyes.

The sky today
is milling with invisible survivors.
From the shaft we wave.

1970s

Separation

We with our vagrant language
we with our incorrigible accents
and another word for milk
we who come by train
and embrace on platforms
we and our wagons
we whose voice in our absence
is framed on a bedroom wall
we who share everything
and nothing –
this nothing which we break in two
and wash down with a gulp
from the only bottle,
we whom the cuckoo
taught to count,
into what currency
have they changed our singing?
What in our single beds
do we know of poetry?

We are experts in the presents
both wrapped ones
and the others left surreptitiously.
Before leaving we hide our eyes our feet our backs.
What we take is for the luggage rack.
We leave our eyes behind
in the window frames and mirrors
we leave our feet behind
we leave our backs behind
in the mortar of the walls
and the doors hung on their hinges.

The door closed behind us
and the noise of the wagon wheels.

We are experts too in taking.
We take with us anniversaries
the shape of a fingernail
the silence of the child asleep
the taste of your celery
and your word for milk.

What in our single beds
do we know of poetry?

Single track, junction and
marshalling yards
read out loud to us.
No poem has longer lines
than those we have taken.
Like horsedealers we know how
to look a distance in the mouth
and judge its pain by its teeth.

With mules, on foot
by airliners and lorries
in our hearts
we carry everything,
harvests, coffins, water,
oil, hydrogen, roads,
flowering lilac and
the earth frown into the mass grave.

We with our bad foreign news
and another word for milk
what in our single beds
do we know of poetry?

We know as well as the midwives
how women carry children
and give birth,
we know as well as the scholars
what makes a language quiver.

Our freight.
The bringing together of what has been parted
makes a language quiver.
Across millennia and the village street
through tundra and forests
by farewells and bridges
towards the city of our child
everything must be carried.

We carry poetry
as the cattle trucks of the world
carry cattle.
Soon in the sidings
they will sluice them down.

1984/85

Places

Amsterdam

high up
    close to the bed of the sky
flounders are making
    ash fall like snow

gulls wheeling in
    smaller
        and smaller
                circles
lower their feet in flight
    to walk upon the flakes

in the paintings of Malevich
white is space made substantial

at each crossing the traffic lights
change from white
    to white

the giant flakes dissolve
    on the brown arm of the canal
        raised imperceptibly higher

ice contracts   the cold huddle together

when winters were still new to me
I held the fingers of one hand
    cold sticks of ache
        in the palm of my other

an empty white dray
    drawn by a grey horse
        follows a tram

the snow is filling the dray

1972

At Remaurian

for Sven, Romaine and Anya

I

Down from the mountain
The yellow of knife-handles
Past the olives
To the age of my mill
Wherein stone pacifies stone
With the oil of season after season
And a man sleeping
May be woken
By the stillness of my wheel.

II

A butterfly disturbs a grain
The grain another
Till there is such friction in the dust
The sky spills its blue milk
On the stones that have conceived

A day is born

Down the precipitous gaze of its opened eyes
The trees are led.

III

At the nocturnal level of the hand
Herbs must always grow
Leaf of my leaf
But early enough
And upright
Following in the wake of the trees
I have felt against the vein of my wrist
Webs breaking
Till every connection of the night is severed
And single I step forward to become
The honey-coloured fleck
On the iris of the first comer's eye.

IV

Seen naked the day rises
Till its eyes can probe
Beyond the walls on which lizards tattooed
Beat the rate of my pulse
Through groves so ancient
No desire of mine
Can be separate from its origin
In the glance of a man
A millennium ago
Down erogenous slopes
Where poised boulders await
The staring
Behind a cataract of pleasure
Over hills as patient as the unconceived
To that horizon
Which miles moisten in their welcome
And sight divides.

V

Let the drawing stand up
And every dot
Yield a line
As the field that was sown
Is raised by its crop
And my nipple by the slow-growing tree.

Let the drawing stand up
And make of my legs
The legs of the table
On which this land is
Laid out like a towel
And placed like a bowl
Awaiting its water.

Let the drawing stand up
And its weight bear down
Till every line is opened
And the distance they cover
Is the format of the sky
Above my lover.

Let the drawing stand up
And pour from its lip
All that can turn my wheel.

VI

As I climb
The mountain sweats

The heart beats faster.
Stones drip
To trickle down the spine

In the valley
The mouth of the river like a rumour
Whispers water in the ear of the fields

Before it is dark
From this summit my mountain
You must descend me.

VII

Cover me cover me
That I am spread as the whiteness of rock
And no ignorance remains in the light
When every organ
With its workings is displayed
Letting spermatozoa and egg
Be as evident to sight
As pairing butterflies
The glance of whose wings
It will then be too late
For this gazing sun
Ever to misinterpret.

VII

Sweet clamour
And the voice of a child
In the torrent of my cries
Helped you name
The unnameable colour
Of my womb
Since from my bough
My leaves then unfolded
And I pursued
With my tongue
The lineage of your wood.

IX

Stones still warm
Taste of your hands

Length and height lose
Their terraced scale

The light descends to the level sea

With the waters of the robe I do not wear

The dark examines us
By touch alone.

1962/63

Alpage

Murmuring river
clasps the mist
for a moment more.
The peaks are signing on
the sky.
Stop and hear
the milking machines
designed to suck like calves.
In the first heat
the forested hills calculate
their steepness.
The lorry driver is taking the road
to the pass which leads
surprisingly
with its own familiarity
to another homeland.
Soon the grass will be
warmer
than the cows' horns.
The astounding comes
towards us
outrider of death and birth.

1980s

Robert Jorat

This morning Robert
I polished my black boots
to be correct and neat
for your adieu

Your coffin was small
and one of your granddaughters
lit the candles
for its four corners

You taught me
the dying art
of sharpening a scythe
with a hammer

At your grave side
I see your thumb nail
testing the blade
thin as foil

With the years you grew frailer
and I tapped
to draw the steel
each year thinner

Yet afterwards
you always took the blade
and with a short hammer
corrected my ineptitudes

Next June
I must sharpen the scythe alone
and for you I will try Robert
to make it sharper than my grief

1996

Forest

Each pine at dusk
lodges the bird
of its voice
perpendicular and still
the forest
indifferent to history
tearless as stone
repeats
in tremulous excitement
the ancient story
of the sun going down

1980s

Winter Loss

against the white
small birds dart furtive as mice
a wooden ladder against the white
acquires the look of leather

a madman finds in the snow
a plank of wood so knotted
it can warm the knuckles of his hand

on a white face trees are scratched
around a white basin a few hairs are left

the white closes its case of snow
and locks it with two iron cattle.

1969

Ladle

Pewter pock-marked
moon of the ladle
rising above the mountain
going down into the saucepan
serving generations
steaming
dredging what has grown from seed
in the garden
thickened with potato
outliving us all
on the wooden sky
of the kitchen wall

Serving mother
of the steaming pewter breast
veined by the salts
fed to her children
hungry as boars
with the evening earth
engrained around their nails
and bread the brother
serving mother

Ladle
pour the sky steaming
with the carrot sun
the stars of salt
and the grease of the pig earth
pour the sky steaming
ladle
pour soup for our days
pour sleep for the night
pour years for my children

1977

Ladder

The uprights are pine
the rungs are ash
between each rung
the grass of months is pressed
hard as a saddle

At the foot of the ladder
on her back
belly distended
like a grey risen loaf
a dead ewe
legs in the air
thin as the legs
of a kitchen chair
she strayed yesterday
ate too much lucerne
which fermenting
burst her stomach
the first snow
falls on her grey wool
a vole in the dark
systematically
eats the ear on the ground
at daybreak two crows
haphazardly peck
the gums of the teeth
her frosted eyes are open

Every ladder
is lightheaded
on the topmost rung
the seeds have flowered
into the colours of the world
and two butterflies white
like the notes of an accordion
pursuing
touching
parting
climb the blue sky

Far above the ladder's head
instantaneously
their white wings change into blue
and they disappear
like the dead

Descending
and ascending
this ladder
I live

1980s

Hay

The flowers in her hair
wet in the morning
are dry by ten

Her apron clings
stones like hands
press in her pocket

Tomorrow
the scythes will gasp
as her clothes fall down

On this slope she'll lie
hands on its shoulder
feet on the road below

Gathered in lines
her cocks will crouch
like couples in the moonlight

Next day in the sun
she'll walk on her hands
to get as dry as fire

Combed by the women
lifted by men
she'll ride the carts

Front wheels locked
with a pole through their spokes
I'll take her down

And when I pack her
second wife under my roof
my sweat will blind me.

1980s

Death of La Nan M.

in memory of Lauren Malgrand

When she could no longer
prepare mash for the chickens
or peel potatoes
for the soup
she lost her appetite
even for bread
and scarcely ate

He was painting himself
black on the branches
to watch the crows
who no longer flew high
but kept to the earth

Smaller than the stove
she sat by the window
where outside the leeks grow

By the wood stack
– the hillsides of brushwood
she had carried on her back –
he crouched and became
the chopping block

Her daughter-in-law
fed the chickens
put wood in the stove

At night he reclined on each side
of the black fire
burning her bed
what she asked him was his opposite?
Milk he answered with appetite

Lining the kitchen
family and neighbours followed
her fight for breath

High up the mountain
he pissed on
snow and ice
to melt the stream

She found it easier if
she laid her head
on the arm of the chair

His urine was the shape
of an icicle
and as colourless

In her hand
she held a handkerchief
to dab her mouth
when it needed wiping

On his black mirror
there was never breath

The guests as they left
kissed the crown of her head
and she knew them
by their voices

He trundled out a barrow
overturned it
on the frozen dungheap
its two legs still warm

The seventy-third anniversary
of her marriage night
she spent
huddled in the kitchen
from time to time calling her son
she called him by his surname
who rocked on his slippered feet
like a bear

One mistake you made
Death did not joke like a drunk
You should not have grown old

I was not a thief she replied

Dead she looked as tall
laid out on her bed
in dress and boots
as when a bride
but her right shoulder
was lower than the left
on account of all
she had carried

At her funeral
the village saw the soft snow
bury her
before the gravedigger

1977

Village Maternity

The mother puts
      the newborn day
           to her breast

turnips
      like skulls
           are heaped
                house high

before the blood has been washed
            from the legs of the sky

1976

They Are The Last

for Beverly

Behind her tongue
with its language of grass
and passion for salt,
behind the heavy tongue
deft nevertheless
as a blind man's hand,
a cow in good health chews
approximately fifty times
before re-swallowing the cud.

It appears the animals
Beverly
are emigrating: their America
the constellations in the sky:
Lizard, Lion, Great Bear,
Ram, Bull, Crow,
Hare…
Perhaps the more prudent
like the agouti
have chosen the milky way.

Put your ear to her flank
and you will hear
the tide of her four stomachs.
Her second, like a net,
has the name of a constellation:
Reticulum. Her third,
the Psalterium, is like
the pages of a book.

When she falls sick
and lacks the will to chew
her four stomachs fall
silent as a hive in winter.

Each year more animals depart.

Only pets and carcasses remain,
and the carcasses living or dead
are from birth
ineluctably and invisibly
turned into meat.
'I believe it's completely feasible,'
said Bob Rust
of Iowa State University,
'to specifically design
an animal for hamburger.'

Elsewhere
the animals of the poor
die with the poor
from protein insufficiency.

When fetched from the pastures
the cattle bring into the cool stable
the heat of the orchard
and the hot breath of wild garlic.

To clean out the cowshed
scatter a little of
the mare's dung
it absorbs their shit
liquid as springtime
and green with grass.

And fasten them well tonight
bed them with beech leaves
Beverly
they are the last.

Now that they have gone
it is their endurance we miss.
Unlike the tree
the river or the cloud
the animals had eyes
and their glance
was permanence.

It was the same fox for ever and ever.
To kill him
was to drag him
momentarily
from the earth
of his eternity.

Flies and crows
when devouring the dead sheep
began with the eyes.
Yet the ewe
had already lambed
her permanence.

The buzzard circled
biding his everlasting time
as repeatedly
as the mountain.

Out of the single night
came the day's look,
with its wary animal glance
to every side.

The animals flowed like their milk.
Now that they have gone
it is their endurance we miss.

'The breeding sow,' it is said,
'should be thought of and treated
as a valuable piece of machinery
whose function
is to pump out baby pigs'

Yet sometimes
when you are pouring
from the white jug,
the milk
reminds me of the geese
who like dogs
guarded the house.

2008

Snow

The covering bird
who came in November
to build a nest
with forests of pine
orchards roofs and fences
is going to vanish.

His white wings lie
discarded
on the green sky
whose stars are crocuses.

Tomorrow
his last seed
will disappear like salt into meat
and soon I'll saw the wood
he broke
when he came to fuck our winter.

1980

Potatoes

The cock crows
      the soil its black feathers spread
          claws its stone
             and lays its eggs

Don't lift them too soon
      they give light off
          through their moon skin
             to the dead

During the snow
      heaped in cellars
          they gravely offer
             body to the soup

When they fail
      the plough has no meat
          and men starve like the great bear
             in the winter night

1980s

Solitary Shepherd's Moonrise

On that horizon
engraved on each day
like the crack in the coffee bowl
cows become the size they were
when I was four

To the north of the cows
graze the rocks
named the Tall Ones
there where the moon rises
when all has been done

First a pink halo
the colour of the dress
worn at a dance by her
father my father they say
went barefoot for

The dress has no hem my son

Then a lake of pale skin
there where the sons swam
one last night
and the boots they left on the bank
never to climb again

The horizon opens like a mouth my son

Slowly slowly
the bone white head is born
your body of light
slips trailing out
from where my god you came.

1980

Soave

On her bicycle she rides
beside a dead canal
reciting the lines by Carducci
she learnt last week at school
on this canal when I was young
barges crossed so close
it was like a kiss...

Kalemegdan: Beograd

Beside the battlements
where the living defenders
joined the dead
still fighting
to defend their walls
lovers today
fondle and embrace
as the Sava takes
the arm of the Danube
to go together
into the bliss of some black sea
here the city was built
here children will be born

1971

Sunset

Like a trout
our mountain basks
in the setting sun

as the light drains
the trout dies
its mouth open

the night
with its wings of spruce
flies the mountain

to the dead

1980s

Herdsman

The darkness of night is
       far from the living
           as granite
5:00am. November

On the panes
       minus fifteen grow
           flowers of ice
5:00am. December

The morning stove is dead and
       silent as the wood
           of the frozen trees
5:00am. January

On waking sleep solicits
       another visit
           to her summers
5:00am. February

Declining he farts
       lights the fire goes out
           with his churn
5:30am.

1980s

Terrain

I'm going
       going
to lie on the earth
           the earth
will lay back both her ears
and with my forearm
             forearm
between them
the fingers of my hand
will play
      play around
with her muzzle
        kept cool
by a wind from
God knows where.

2000

My Love

My Coney

My Coney whose symmetry is
beyond the protractor's so precise
three hundred and sixty degrees,
Island sea whose green patterns
no diver can measure
save with his own desire,
Wayward dancer who has left
swinging white every gate
she has paused to open
(not even in her palms
can the meadows she has walked upon
be delineate),
Bird of whose folded wings
no normal ornithologist
can gauge the span,
Soothsayer whose fingerprints
chart an arabia
irredeemable as the phoenix,
Do not submit
to any corollary
but, my love, elude me still.

1952

28 November 1961

for Anya

No door can close today
on what it closed before.

You bore me a daughter
As ships for their sailors
Bear houses at evening.

You made two
of one whom I know.

I held your hand
to fill the night.

From Dieppe

for Beverly

On the table
under the lamp
are three pebbles
I brought from Dieppe

Often when I eat
drink coffee or talk
they interrupt
the trains of my thought

One is green coloured
long and thick
and it lunges on the cloth
like a fish

The second is brown
and open with a tongue
when I first saw it
I thought of a muzzle

The third is oval
dark grey in net of white
regular and haphazard
it reminds me of nothing

When the stones interrupt
I put out my hand
to touch
what I find in them

I adjust the fish
so that I can see
its eye
and the thrust of its tail

I place
my little finger
between the jaws
of the brown animal.

The third pebble I pick up
hold deliberately
and place back on the table
so that

it looks to me like itself

1974

Street Scene

The light evening
Like your fingers at night
Never stops

By the unlit traffic-light
Our laughter crosses the road

Under your arms
April

Later in the peach stone's
Red hammock
We'll lie in the halved fruit
The knife our two names.

1980s

5am

You know of
what I do not
rapids
buttons
toccatinas
a certain way of cooking lentils
the outlook of metals

I know your secrets
keep them under my tongue
our binding is ignorance

When the book closes
the pages learn
and a pillow reads
what is in our heads

1980s

Learning by Heart

My heart born naked
was swaddled in lullabies.
Later alone it wore
poems for clothes.
Like a shirt
I carried on my back
the poetry I had read.

So I lived for half a century
until wordlessly we met.

From my shirt on the back of the chair
I learn tonight
how many years
of learning by heart
I waited for you.

1980s

Old Love Poem

The hay
smelt of how
the sky loved the earth.
You were the pain in my ribs
aching
from the carts unloaded.

The dead
were filling a doorway
with the view beyond.
You were the house
the candle under the plum tree
and my eternity.

1980s

Hendrickye by Rembrandt

A necklace hangs loose across her breasts,
And between them lingers –
      yet is it a lingering

and not an incessant arrival? –
the perfume of forever.
A perfume as old as sleep,
as familiar to the living as to the dead.

1970s

Poem for Beatrice

Continually mists change my size
Only territories on a map are measured
The sounds I make are made elsewhere
I am enveloped in the astonishing silence of my breasts
I plait my hair into sentences
Never let loose
I walk where I wish
My cuffs admit my wrists alone
Break
Break the astonishing silence of my breasts.

1960s

Distant Village

The mountains are pitiless
the rain is melting the snow
it will freeze again.

In the café two strangers
play the accordion
and the room of men are singing.

Tunes are filling
the sacks of the heart
the troughs of the eyes.

Words are filling
the stalls
which bellow between the ears.

Music shaves the jowls
loosens the joints,
the only cure for rheumatism.

Music cleans the nails
softens your hands
scours the callouses.

A room full of men
come from drenched cattle,
diesel oil, the eternal shovel,

are caressing
the air of a love song
with sweetened hands.

Mine have left my wrists
and are crossing the mountains
to find your breasts.

In the café two strangers
play the accordion
the rain is melting the snow.

1986

Island

On your island
does the night fall later?
Am I walking a little ahead of you
so that no snake will bite
your sandaled foot?

The balance is never made.
This is why the stars are silent
offering no account.

How to measure
a season
against
the calendar of your absence?

How to measure
the stream
of my tangled light
in the mountain
of what has been
and will be?

The balance is never made.

Yet in the night your eyes and mine
sounding one another
show no trace of vertigo.

1980s

Side by Side

The white coral
threaded by the winter ocean
will never be worn
as necklace
by you or I
whilst we remain
on this side
side by side
of that origin
which calved time
and parted winter from summer
but sleeping together
we precede the amoeba.

1990s

Lovers in a Park

The magnolia is in flower

In the old conservatory
      pensioners are playing cards

The magnolia is in flower

A gardener drives a rotary mower
      without its blades

The magnolia is in flower

Blowing last years leaves
      from the flowering beds

The magnolia is in flower

To lift me from the earth
      place your hands far below

The magnolia is in flower

So that my roots come away
      with their soil.

1972

Likeness

Who is drawing me
between pencil and paper?

One day I shall judge the likeness
but she who judges
will not be the woman who now
so expectantly poses.

I am what I am.

What I am like is how you see me.

1960s

Make Again

Slowly the small hours draw
                    dawn from its scabbard

his skin tastes of salt
waves break over a crest
lifting pebbles
on to a rock
the undertow sucks them
from the rock   on to the bed
skin tastes of his salt
waves break over a crest
lifting pebbles

the dawn beheads reason
                    lays its blade across
                    a shoulder of madness

the madness to cut
        blocks of breath
        between sea and sun
        and make again
        a voyage like a tower

1970s

Insomnia

not I
but the lion sleeps
when I move
he stirs

I between the bars
extend my hand
to touch your face

in the head
like a boulder
upon his paws
he
dreams.

1973/74

My Honey

The apple trees are barking
the beestings on my scalp
mark the rage of the swarm
hold, my honey, your sweetness.

The sky is pressing its thumbs
into my eyes
his constellations are fleeing
hold, my honey, your sweetness.

The endless rain
desiring the mountains as sand
is preparing me for bed
hold, my honey, your sweetness.

1970s

And our faces

When I open my wallet
to show my papers
pay money
or check the time of a train
I look at your face.

The flower's pollen
is older than the mountains
Aravis is young
as mountains go.

The flower's ovules
will be seeding still
when Aravis then aged
is no more than a hill.

The flower in the heart's
wallet, the force
of what lives us
outliving the mountain.

And our faces, my heart, brief as photos.

1980s

A View of Delft

In that town,
across the water
where all has been seen
and the bricks are cherished like sparrows,
in that town like a letter from home
read again and again in a port,
in that town with its library of tiles
and its addresses recalled by Johannes Vermeer
who died in debt,
in that town across the water
where the dead take the census
and there are no vacant rooms
for his gaze occupies them all,
where the sky is waiting
to have news of a birth,
in that town which pours from the eyes
of those who left it,
there
between two chimes of the morning,
when fish are sold in the square
and the maps on the walls
show the depth of the sea,
in that town
I am preparing for your arrival.

1980s

Kerchief

In the morning
folded with its wild flowers
washed and ironed
it takes up little space in the drawer.

Shaking it open
she ties it round her head.

In the evening she pulls it off
and lets it fall
still knotted to the floor.

On a cotton scarf
among printed flowers
a working day
has written its dream.

1981

The Leather of Love

Weathered as gate posts
by departures
and the white ghosts
of the gone,
wrapped in tarpaulins,
we talk of passion.
Our passion's the saline
in which hides are hung
to make from a hinge of skin
the leather of love.

1987

Sky

in the first silence
I heard myself cry

sky lay beside earth

to listen to their rain
I learnt not to cry

a ladder on its shoulder
sky

we are making love

with its fingers
places petals of itself

in the highest branches
sky

1990s

Acknowledgements

Thanks are due to the publishers of the following, where some of these poems first appeared in book form:

Permanent Red (1960), *G.* (1972), *A Seventh Man* (with Jean Mohr, 1975), *Pig Earth* (1979), *Once in Europa* (1983), *And Our Faces, My Heart, Brief as Photos* (1984), *Pages of the Wound* (1994), *Keeping a Rendezvous* (1992), *Lilac and Flag* (1992), *The Sense of Sight* (1993), *Another Way of Telling* (with Jean Mohr, 1995), *Why Look at Animals?* (2009) and *Le louche et autres poèmes* (with Yves Berger, 2012).